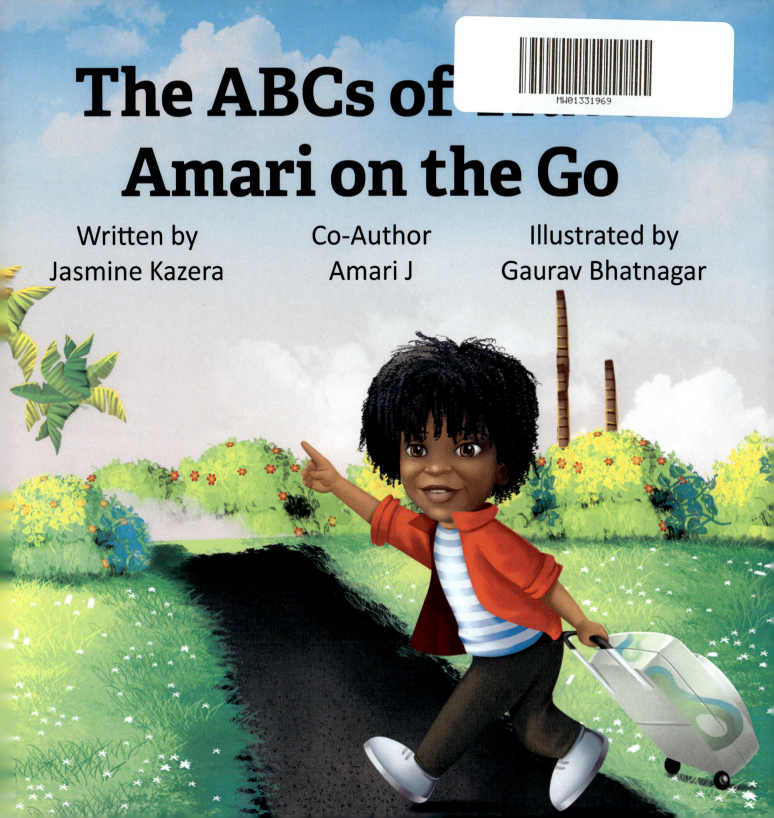

This Book belongs to

_____

© 2022 Jasmine Kazera All Rights Reserved

No portion of this book may be reproduced or transmitted in any form or by any means, Electronic or mechanical, including photocopying, recording, or by any information storage and retrieval system,
without the permission in writing from the publisher.

For permissions contact: amarionthegobooks@gmail.com
ISBN: 979-8-9852150-0-7

Illustrated and designed by Gaurav Bhatnagar
www.ePublishingexperts.com

This book is dedicated to
Uncle Sonny aka The Smartest Man in the World
and Mommom Madeline, My First Best Friend.

Aa Airplane

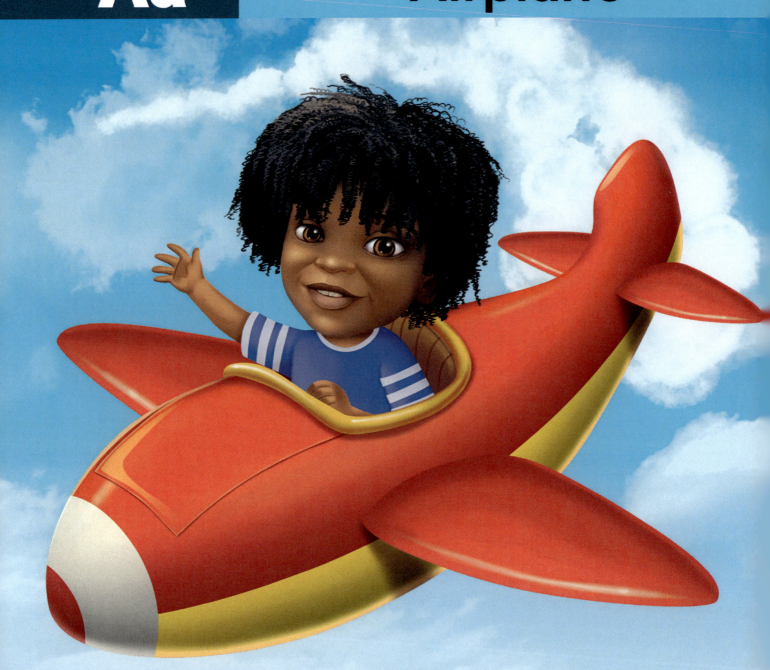

Bb Beach

Cc

Cruise

Dd Destination

Ee Explore

Ff Food

Gg Globe

Hh Hotel

Ii

Island

Jj Journey

Kk Keepsake

Ll

Luggage

Mm

Map

Nn National Park

Oo Outdoors

Pp Passport

Qq Quest

Rr

Relax

Ss Safari

Tt

Tourist

Uu Umbrella

Vv

Vacation

Ww

Waterfall

Xx

eXcited

Yy

Yacht

Zz Zoo

Aa	Bb	Cc	Dd
Ee	Ff	Gg	Hh
Ii	Jj	Kk	Ll
Mm	Nn	Oo	Pp
Qq	Rr	Ss	Tt
Uu	Vv	Ww	Xx
	Yy	Zz	

About the Author

Jasmine Kazera has always loved to read and write. She remembers going on vacations with her family and reading her favorite books while they drove for hours from one destination to the next. As she got older, traveling became another one of her passions.

Her son, Amari J., became her co-author and inspiration behind creating "Amari on the Go" children's books. Together, they hope to introduce the world of travel to young children all over the world. They hope to teach people that travel is attainable and show how much fun it can be to learn about new places and cultures.

Made in the USA
Middletown, DE
03 April 2025